THE MENTOR WITH LYNN MARKETING SERIES

BOOK 3

DROP YOUR SIZZLE

How to use drop cards to build your business

BY

Lynn Leach

Drop Your Sizzle is designed to help you understand the importance of having a drop card to aid you in lead generation and to help you utilize that sizzle line to grow your business. A sizzle line will help in the sorting and sifting process, as now you will only be speaking with individuals who are interested in having you contact them. So a sizzle line generates a more qualified prospect as opposed to a generic lead. The drop card that advertises the sizzle line will help you generate leads in any area you desire to work in. This is the third book of The MENTOR WITH LYNN Marketing Series. The series focuses on marketing training for network marketers.

PLEASE REVIEW THIS BOOK ON AMAZON.COM.

It will help me make the next version better. I appreciate your input.

Peace, Health and Prosperity.

Income Disclaimer: This book contains business strategies, marketing methods and other business advice that, regardless of the authors results and experience, may not produce the same results (or any results) for you. The author and publisher make absolutely no guarantee, expressed or implied, that by following the advice below you will make any money or improve current profits, as there are several factors and variables that come into play regarding any given business.

Primarily, results will depend on the nature of the product or business model, the conditions of the marketplace, the experience of the individual, the commitment, consistency and discipline of the individual, and situations and elements that are beyond your control.

As with any business, you assume all risk related to investment and money based on your own discretion and at your own potential expense.

Liability Disclaimer: By reading this book or the documents it offers, you assume all risks associated with using the advice given, with a full understanding that you, solely, are responsible for anything that may occur as a result of putting this information into action in any way, and regardless of your interpretation of the advice.

You further agree that the author and publisher cannot be held responsible in any way for the success or failure of your business as a result of the information provided by this book. It is your responsibility to conduct your own due diligence regarding the safe and successful operation of your business if you intend to apply any of this information in any way to your business operations.

In summary, you understand that that the author and publisher make absolutely no guarantees regarding income as a result of applying this information, as well as the fact that you are solely responsible for the results of any action taken on your part as a result of any given information.

In addition, for all intents and purposes you agree that our content is to be considered "for entertainment purposes only". Always seek the advice of a professional when making financial, tax or business decisions.

Any statements pertaining to health or health related products in the contents of this book are provided for educational purposes only and are not intended to diagnose, treat, cure, or prevent any disease or health condition. The information provided herein should not be considered as a substitute for the advice of a medical doctor or other healthcare professional.

ABOUT THE AUTHOR

Lynn Leach has been involved with the industry of MLM/network marketing and direct sales for 45 years. She is a retired Pastor (as retired as any Pastor can be!), and owns Common Scents Health Research and Wellness Centers and Leach Publishing. You can reach Lynn at <u>724-292-8481</u> or email her at <u>pastorlynn@comcast.net</u> and her wellness center website is <u>www.LynnLeach.com</u>

Her corporate website with Paid2Save is:
<u>www.Paid2Save.com/pastorlynn</u>

and her Viral Card is:

http://viralcard.paid2save.com/72454

Her training site is

www.mentorwithlynn.com

WHAT ARE DROP CARDS AND HOW DO I USE THEM?

Are you looking for a way to EXPLODE your business? Do you feel you are disciplined, committed and willing to work consistently to build your business? There is a PROVEN way to market that will provide you with a source of fresh, hot prospects on a daily basis. This marketing strategy builds on a sizzle line and utilizes what we call **DROP CARDS**.

Before I go into explaining what drop cards are and how you use them, I want to tell you about a very good friend and colleague who actually used this strategy to build a million dollar business.

He and his wife made a decision to put out 2,000 cards per day. They were buying cards 500,000 at a time. They were determined to work the numbers and get the cards out – and they literally built a million dollar a year business for themselves. They were disciplined enough to be consistent in working at getting those cards out daily. They set their goal and then committed to getting it done.

So what are the drop cards, and exactly how do you use them? Drop cards are advertising cards that are about the size of a business card. They urge prospects to call your sizzle line number to learn more about your product, service or business opportunity. You must have a sizzle line number set up with a compelling message that will peak their interest, and motivate them to leave you their contact details to get more information from you. If you need help with understanding how to set up a sizzle line, please refer to Book 2 in The **MENTOR WITH LYNN MARKETING SERIES:** *SIZZLE YOUR WAY TO SUCCESS*.

You leave your drop cards anywhere you go: at the dentist's office, the doctor's office, the grocery store, the theater, the gym...virtually **EVERYWHERE YOU GO!** You can place them in rest rooms, on newspaper stands, gasoline pumps, cash registers and check-out counters, or simply hand them out to people at the bank, checkout counter, restaurant, etc. Place the drop cards in the smoking areas of buildings — people are just standing or sitting there for several minutes with virtually nothing to do. Go to the library or a newsstand and flip through a few books and place a card in each book or magazine. For gas pumps, place your cards in a zip lock baggie and duct tape the bag to the gas pump. I was in Raleigh, North Carolina for A Mind, Body Spirit Trade Show, and a gal was really using her brain. I always place the cards in the stall...on a shelf...but this gal taped her cards all over the wall above the sink and mirrors and hand dryers. So you could easily pull one off and tuck it in your purse or pocket. And they were all at eye level – so you couldn't miss them.

Another good idea is to get a business card magnet. Pull the backing off of it and stick it to the back of a Lucite business card holder. Whenever you park your car, stick the holder on the car with your drop cards in it. Place a sign that says **TAKE ONE** with an arrow pointing to the cards.

Wherever you place them, people will see the cards, pick them up and **DIAL YOUR SIZZLE LINE**

NUMBER. Bingo...you have a hot prospect interested in having you contact them. How easy is that!?!

I would suggest to you that you determine how many cards you will put out on a daily basis. Put them in your pocket, your purse or briefcase. Keep a supply in your car. And then make sure that you do not stop passing them out until you have reached your daily goal.

My friend and his wife used to go to sporting events and hit all of the cars. Now if you are putting the cards on cars...do NOT put them on the windshield. Place them in the window of the door on the driver's side of the vehicle. My friend's wife used to go to car garages and stop on each floor, park the car and hit all of the cars. And she did this with an infant strapped to her back! She had determination. She had desire. And she was **COMMITTED!** One of my team members placed them on cars at a restaurant when she was visiting another state. She got a call and sold the gentleman a $15,000 package in a travel company we were in.

This is simply **ADVERTISING.** Exposure is the key to success. So set your daily goal and just get the cards out.

WHERE CAN I GET THEM?

The Drop Card is the first impression your prospect has with your business, and first impressions many times are the deciding factor between whether or not that person calls your sizzle line and leaves a name and number. If you want to attract top-quality prospects, you are more likely to do it with professional-looking Drop Cards than with a cheap Drop Card. Keep it professional and don't be penny wise and dollar foolish. It is worth it to invest in great cards, as you want to maximize your time and efforts and get the most prospects from your work as possible. Remember, you want to attract prospects, get them to pick the card up and then peak their curiosity enough to get them to call the number. So you want the best card you can afford.

There are 3 ways to get your cards. You can order them from a company that specializes in drop cards, or you can design and print them yourself. I will give you adequate information so you can choose to do either.

First, let's talk about copy. **KEEP IT SIMPLE -- LESS IS MORE!** The General rule is: Don't cram too much information on your card, because the less copy you have -- the better the card will produce.

Now let's talk about the color of the card stock they are printed on. Bright Yellow or Florescent Orange or Green paper catches your prospects' attention and causes them to pick up better than any other color. Yellow out-performs white by 30% and florescent colors out-performs bright yellow by 82%! Choose your colors wisely.

There are 2 types of printing, flat printing and raised letter printing. If your budget allows its, go with the raised letter printing.

When considering ink colors, blue ink on yellow paper is more attractive and is more professional than black. Two ink colors (red and blue ink) creates better results, but two colors do not look good on bright florescent paper, so only use one color of ink if you have selected a florescent color card stock.

That should give you enough information should you chose to design and print your own drop cards. And it should prepare you for ordering cards from any company.

Let's take a look at some of the offers out there. A lot of these are really clever. Keep in mind that you will only have a fleeting moment for their eyes to catch your card. Their eyes will only have seconds to convey the message to the brain so it can send the message of curiosity to the hand to pick up the card.

One of the most intriguing cards is the folded money card. There are several places you can order them from. And the selection of cards with compelling messages is getting better every day.

Be willing to invest in the quality of your Drop Cards. The long term and short term dividends far outweigh the few extra pennies it costs to do them right.

Here are some sites to start you off with, but you can also just do a search online for drop cards.

http://www.dollarcardmarketing.com/order-cards.html

I like to leave this one for my waiter or waitress at restaurants.

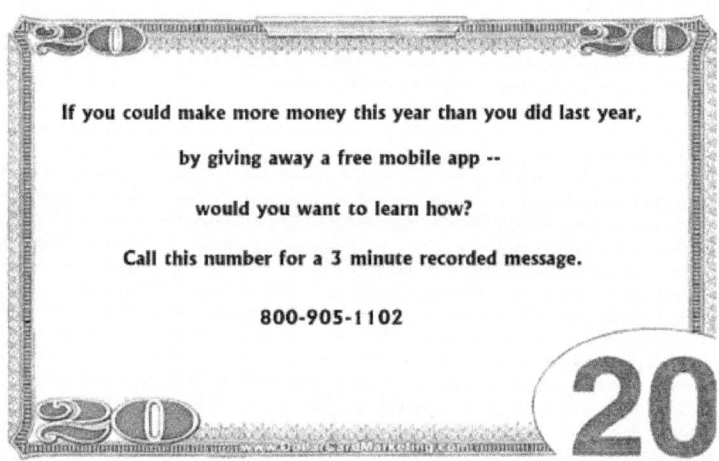

http://www.trickmoney.com/

This is the one I like to use for networking group events. You know how fast they go, and everyone is just trying to collect as many business cards as they can get. You need something unique to catch their eye. This does it for me.

These are additional cards I have not ordered yet, but will be ordering to test at bingo halls and casinos. These are also from http://www.trickmoney.com/

These are wealth cards my husband uses, and we use the car magnet for the back windows of our vehicles from this company. These are from Growth Pro.

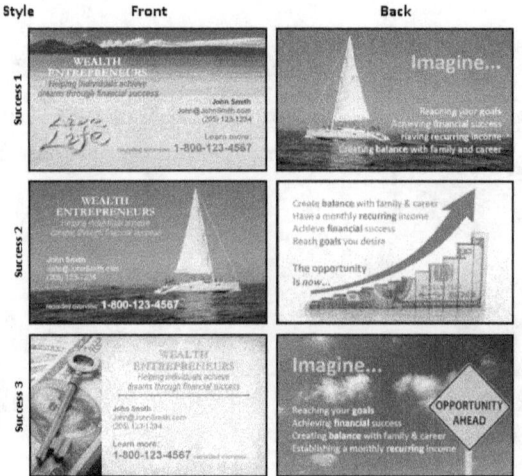

Here are cards specific to my opportunity with Paid2Save, and I have and use all 3

For customers to download the free mobile app:

To use with merchants:

Business opportunity cards:

http://dropcardsusa.com/

This is another company that has the money drop cards. Sometimes they run a pretty good special.

HOW DO I TRACK THEM?

I am big on tracking everything you do. I believe it to just be wisdom. You want to make sure you are maximizing your time, effort and marketing dollars. You need to test different messages and you need to test the places where you drop the cards.

Obviously, some cards and messages will out-perform others. (Please note, this also applies to the actual message on your sizzle line). So you want to make sure that you are constantly tracking and evaluating. Make changes accordingly. Also know that some locations will be better than other locations. Pay attention to the areas you are working.

To test and track your efforts, use a code number on your cards. Have a different code number for different cards. Mix them all together and then pass them out. When you record your message, ask them to also leave the code number on the card they have. Log the code numbers when you retrieve the messages. Then, when you call the prospects, ask where they got the card so you can track the locations.

It is so important to track – work smart...not hard! By monitoring your results, you'll be able to increase your results without

expending more effort or more of your precious time and money.

FOLLOW UP

When someone picks up your drop card, calls your sizzle line and leaves their contact information...YOU NEED TO FOLLOW UP WITH THEM!!!

One of the great lessons in network marketing is, "THE FORTUNE IS IN THE FOLLOW UP". You can do all of the other steps right, but if you do not follow up on the prospects, you will not sell or bring anyone on your team. And, you will not make any money and your business will fail.

You must follow up on the leads. And this should be an easy feat because these are not leads – they are actually prospects.

They want your information.
They are interested in your offer.
They want you to contact them.

They are begging you to call and give them the information. They are handing you their information BECAUSE THEY WANT YOU TO CONTACT THE – HOW EASY IS THAT!?!

Get in the habit of checking your messages daily. Call people as soon as you can, definitely within 24 – 48 hours. Even when you are traveling, the cell phone makes it easy for you to stay in touch with your prospects. Make it a priority to contact them quickly.

Once you contact them, set them up on a live or recorded webinar, or conference call. Schedule a 3 way with your up-line after the event. If you are lucky enough to have a live event you can take them to, please do so.

Stay in touch with your prospects. Get them set up on an automated email campaign. Send them a note and stay in touch by phone. It does take 9 contacts on the average to close a sale. So be persistent.

And please remember that you are in business for yourself, but you are not by yourself...so take advantage of using your up-line for help. They are there for you. You absolutely should be using your up-line for 3 way calls.

WHAT RESULT DO THEY PRODUCE?

Please remember that you must be committed enough to pass out enough cards to get a good handle on the numbers. You can expect to receive 10-15 pre-qualified prospects for every thousand cards you put out, and that would represent anywhere from 2 – 4 hours of your time.

Practice and experience factor in with the results you personally get, because different areas will produce more than others, different cards will produce more than others and different sizzle line messages will produce more than others. Be willing to invest the time to build what you desire.

It takes constant monitoring and tracking to perfect – but this is your business. If you want it to produce a million dollar a year income for yourself, then how much effort are you willing to put into it? Maybe you are not going for a million a year. And that's okay – just put your numbers into perspective.

It's a numbers game. Form a daily habit of getting your cards out. Set your goal for the number you will put out and then stick to it.

You need to determine what you can fit into your budget, and then determine your daily goal – how many will you put out? And yes, I set "DAILY" – because if you are selecting this as one of your marketing strategies, you need to make it a habit. You need to give them out DAILY.

In closing, I just want to say that drop cards are extremely effective in helping you build a local market – or to concentrate on areas you want to develop in. If you constantly advertise with drop cards wherever you go, you will always have a fresh source of interested prospects.

Be DISCIPLINED and CONSISTENT with it – and you will be SUCCESSFUL!

Lynn's other books:

NEW RULES FOR SUCCESS with John Spencer Ellis

DARE TO SUCCEED with Jack Canfield

AGAINST THE GRAIN with Brian Tracy

SUCCESSONOMICS with Steve Forbes

The **WILDERNESS VOYAGE** Devotional Series:

BOOK 1: REBELLION

BOOK 2: MANIPULATION

BOOK 3: DEPRESSION

BOOK 4: FORGIVENESS

BOOK 5: REJECTION

BOOK 6: BITTER ROOTS

BOOK 7: PRIDE

BOOK 8: GREED

The **MENTOR WITH LYNN** Marketing Series:

BOOK 1: CALLING ALL LEADS

BOOK 2: SIZZLE YOUR WAY TO SUCCESS

BOOK 3: DROP YOUR SIZZLE

BOOK 4: SIZZLE SIGNS

BOOK 5: SIZZLING MARKETING IDEAS

BOOK 6: DEVELOPING A POA

BOOK 7: THE NEW MATH FORMULA FOR SUCCESS

BOOK 8: GOALS & VISION BOARDS

BOOK 9: TIME MANAGEMENT

BOOK 10: HOW TO WORK TABLE EVENTS

BOOK 11: YOUR GRAND OPENING

BOOK 12: A SHIFT IN NON PROFIT FUNDRAISING

www.ingramcontent.com/pod-product-compliance
Lightning Source LLC
Chambersburg PA
CBHW071551170526
45166CB00004B/1630